The Celtic Mandala Coloring Book

The Celtic Mandala Coloring Book

Beautiful designs inspired by ancient lore

David Woodroffe

SIRIUS

SIRIUS

This edition published in 2024 by Sirius Publishing, a division of
Arcturus Publishing Limited,
26/27 Bickels Yard, 151–153 Bermondsey Street,
London SE1 3HA

ISBN: 978-1-3988-3680-8
CH011228NT

Printed in China

Introduction

Mandalas are a hugely popular subject for coloring, with their circular shape and repeating patterns making the process of filling them in particularly relaxing. They represent the idea of a spiritual journey in many eastern religions and are used to create a sacred space and induce a trance-like state.

The mandalas in this book are inspired by motifs and symbols from Celtic art. The Celts lived in Scotland, Ireland, Wales, Cornwall, and the Isle of Man, as well as in France and Spain, and over the central portion of continental Europe—and even in European Turkey.

Celtic art, with its recurring motifs, some intertwined into complex and characteristic knots, seems tailor-made for mandalas. You'll also find some typical Celtic animals, including wonderful dragons, intertwined into some of the mandalas.

A wide range of Celtic designs—from classic knots and crosses—have been used as inspiration for these mandalas. You can decide to color them any way you choose—just take a selection of colored pencils, pens, or markers, select a quiet place to work, and start to make your own Celtic-inspired mandalas.

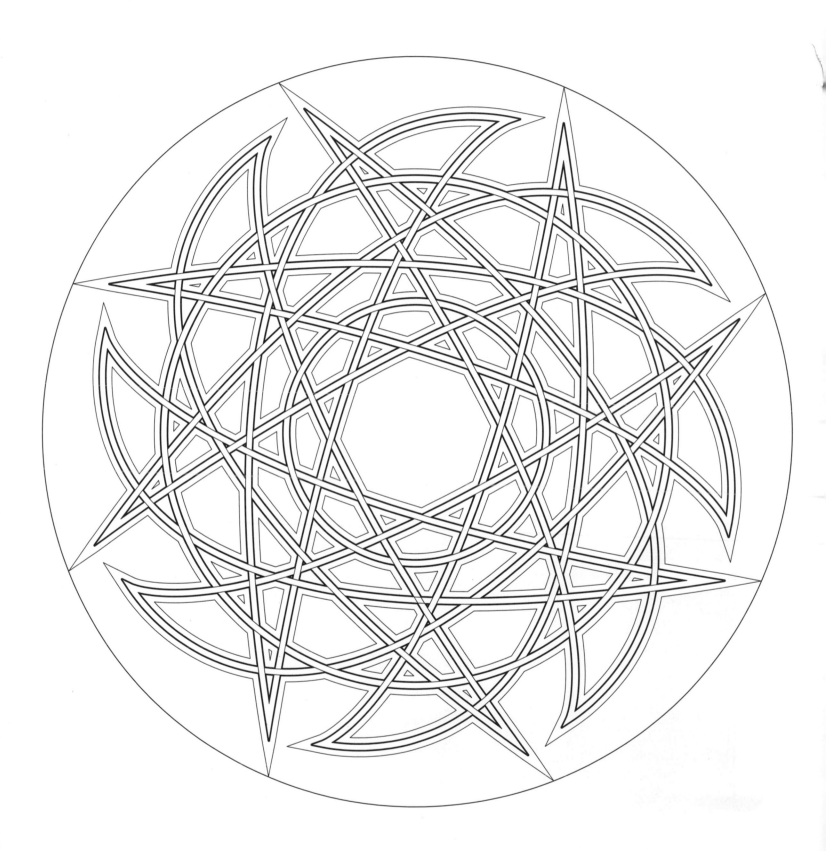

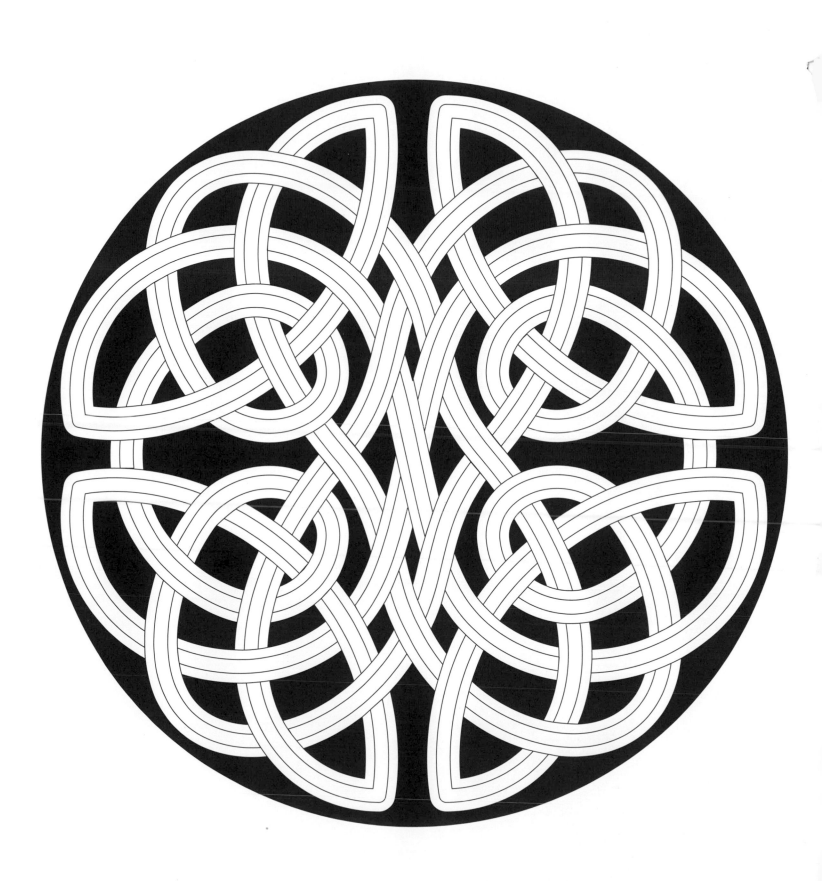

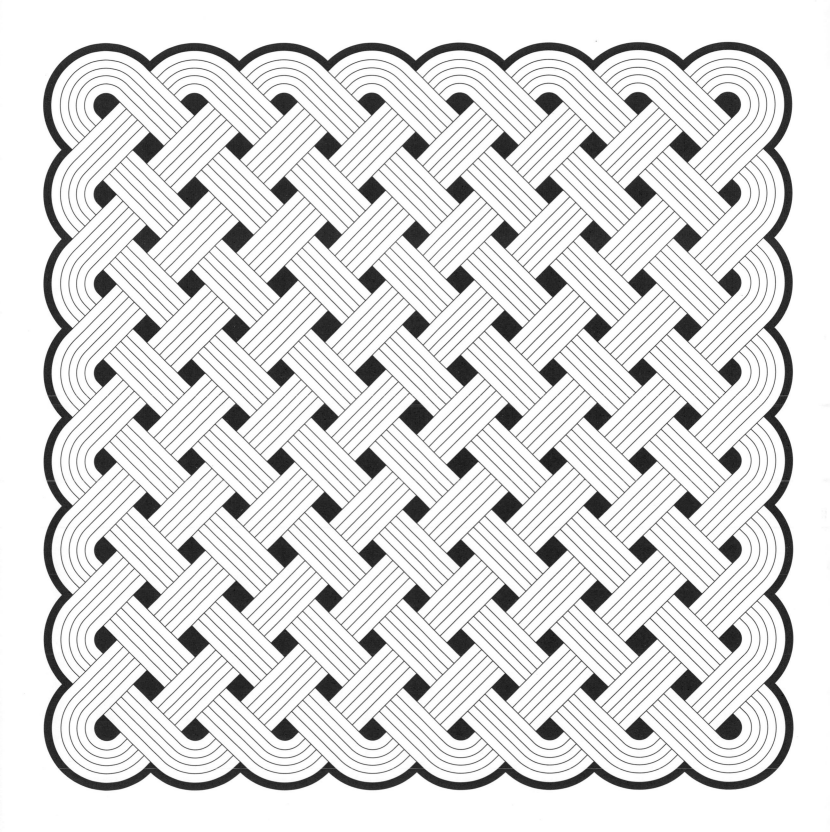